Lighthouse Point

Mark Abbott Memorial lighthouse.

Lighthouse Point

Reflections
on
Monterey Bay History

Frank Perry

GBH PUBLISHING
1982

Published by and available from:
GBH PUBLISHING
Post Office Box 762
Soquel, California 95073

Manufactured in the United States of America

Library of Congress Catalog Card No. 82-90116
ISBN 0-943896-00-2 (hardcover)
ISBN 0-943896-01-0 (softcover)

Typesetting: Typola
Design and Layout: Frank Perry
Printing: Watsonville Press

Illustrations not otherwise credited are by
the author or from the author's collection.

to my parents

Contents

Acknowledgments

It was indeed gratifying to meet so many people who shared my enthusiasm for this project and who eagerly furnished old documents, photographs, and information. I am particularly grateful to the Santa Cruz Historical Society for their grant aiding my research.

I would like to thank the Santa Cruz City Museum; Santa Cruz County Historical Museum; Special Collections, Government Publications, and the Map Library at the University of California McHenry Library in Santa Cruz; U.S. Coast Guard Aids to Navigation Branch, San Francisco; National Maritime Museum, San Francisco; Parks and Recreation Department, Clerk's Office, and Public Works Department of the city of Santa Cruz; Santa Cruz County Recorder's Office; California Coastal Commission; Santa Cruz Port District; National Archives in San Bruno, California, and Washington, D.C.; Santa Cruz Public Library; California Academy of Sciences library, San Francisco; and the *Santa Cruz Sentinel*.

I particularly thank Esther Abbott, Mildred Albronda, Rita Bottoms, Carol Champion, Donald Clark, Ruth Collins, Brian Foss, Starr Gurcke, Jeanie Jordan, Naomi Kraft, Sally Legakis, David Shonman, Paul Stubbs, and Wayne Wheeler for their help.

I am deeply grateful to Dan Harper, Edith Perry, Charles Prentiss, Al Schadel, and Stan Stevens for their many helpful comments and suggestions during final manuscript preparation. I especially thank Stan for generously sharing with me information he discovered about Lighthouse Point during the course of his own research on a related topic.

To these people and the many others who helped, my sincere thanks.

Frank Perry

Introduction

The word *lighthouse* brings several images to mind: tall circular towers on rocky headlands, powerful flashes of light warning mariners of danger, giant glass lenses with brass fittings, and images of crusty old keepers accustomed to the solitude of lighthouse life. Lighthouses have long inspired artists, poets, historians, photographers, and authors. My interest in lighthouses, however, sprouted from quite different images—rather faded images in fact, glued to the warped pages of an aged photograph album. My curiosity grew as I turned each leaf. One of the photos showed several people, their identities unrecorded, smiling from the front steps of a little wooden lighthouse. Others showed a woman, wearing a long dress and bonnet, posed beneath a natural rock arch at the beach. Another photo, warmed to a rich sepia by the many years, showed a horse-drawn buggy skirting the edge of a sea cliff, both the buggy and the waves below blurred by the long camera exposure. These photographs, preserved in a museum collection, launched me into four years of probing the history of one of California's least known lighthouses: the original Santa Cruz light, erected in 1869.

Tragically, a handful of neglected cypress trees and a few ghosts are all that remain of the first Santa Cruz lighthouse. In the 1940s it became the victim of skyrocketing maintenance costs and modern automation. For nearly two decades there was no lighthouse here, only a light on a framework tower. In 1967, through the generosity of Mr. and Mrs. Chuck Abbott of Santa Cruz, a new brick home was built for the light. Now once again a lighthouse graces the northern edge of Monterey Bay.

The study of lighthouses brings together a remarkable variety of disciplines: history, navigation, optics, politics, architecture, and of course the study of the individual triumphs and failures of the people who built and maintained these beacons. The art and science of lighthouses is called *pharology,* a word more commonly used in the nineteenth century. Coined early in that century, the term stems from Pharos, the island from which rose the lighthouse at Alexandria, Egypt, most famous of all lighthouses and one of the seven wonders of the ancient world.

The federal government has been responsible for maintaining our nation's lighthouses almost since the beginning of the United States. On August 7, 1789 the United States Congress passed an act accepting title to the lighthouses then in existence and ordered that money for the maintenance of lighthouses, beacons, and buoys be defrayed out of the U.S. treasury. This was only the ninth act passed by Congress and the first one providing for public work.

Arnold Johnson, in his 1889 book *The Modern Light-House Service,* said: "Science has made wonderful progress during the last quarter of a century, but in no way more than in pharology." Although Mr. Johnson may have been a bit biased (he worked for thirty-nine years as chief clerk for the U.S. Lighthouse Board), his statement nevertheless illustrates the importance placed on lighthouses during that era. That importance is analogous to air traffic control towers today, which likewise guide the flow of people and goods, warning them of danger.

Through the 1800s several different fuels were burned to provide illumination for lighthouses. These included whale oil, colza oil, lard oil, and kerosene. By the end of that century, the use of fire as an illuminating source had reached the peak of perfection. Although the oil lamps were weak by modern standards, powerful lenses focused the light with such precision that its range during clear weather was limited only by the curvature of the earth. Not until the 1920s and 1930s did electric incandescent lights replace oil lamps at most lighthouses. This replacement eventually enabled lighthouses to be automated.

The past few decades have brought many new aids to navigation such as radar, automatic electric beacons, radio signals, and even elaborate satellite networks. Gone now are the uniformed keepers who diligently nurtured the oil lamps through the stormy nights. And gone are many of the lighthouses that once shone brightly over the waters of the Pacific. In the 1940s, when the original Santa Cruz lighthouse was dismantled, there was not the interest in historic preservation that exists now. One would hope our remaining lighthouses along the California coast and elsewhere will not only survive, but will be restored for the pleasure of future generations.

Lighthouses have a special quality to them. Like the great sailing ships they once guided to port, lighthouses are reminders of slower-paced times—reminders of the days of good old mechanical ingenuity before the advent of electronics. Their whitewashed walls of brick and stone were built to defy nature's most violent winds, rains, and ocean waves. Yet lighthouses seem to be in harmony with nature, picturesque additions to the natural landscape.

This book is the story of one point of land—the lighthouses that were built there, the people who lived there, and the changes that took place there. Locals call it Lighthouse Point. It has been called that since the 1870s shortly after the first lighthouse was built. Officially, however, it is called Point Santa Cruz. This name appears on navigational charts, official records, and most maps. It has had still other names. A French nobleman, La Pérouse, who sailed into Monterey

Bay in 1786, mistakenly thought that this was Vizcaíno's "Punta de Año Nuevo." That point is actually located twenty miles to the northwest. A Spanish map done in 1796 by Alberto de Córdoba shows it as "Punta de Lobos." On sea coasts *lobos* is Spanish for sea lions rather than wolves. The point is still famous for its offshore rock which is usually crowded with yelping California sea lions. In fact, in the 1850s and 1860s local residents called it "Seal Rock Point."

One cannot adequately tell the story of a lighthouse without reflecting just a little on its neighboring lighthouses and, for that matter, on the nation's lighthouse system as a whole. Each lighthouse was built as part of a chain of navigational aids, its links carefully designed and arranged to help mariners locate their position along the coast. This book traces the history of Lighthouse Point against the backdrop of America's changing lighthouse system and northern Monterey Bay's changing role as a seaport.

Sea lions on rocks off Lighthouse Point. The nearer rock collapsed in 1960-61. (Santa Cruz Public Library)

Choosing a Site

Monterey Bay, located seventy miles south of San Francisco, is a broad, open bay, some twenty miles wide. Even on maps of the entire United States, Monterey Bay usually stands out, looking like a tiny bite out of the Pacific shoreline. Point Pinos marks the southern boundary between the bay and the Pacific. At the northern boundary lies Point Santa Cruz.

The name Monterey Bay was given to it by the Spanish explorer Sebastián Vizcaíno in 1602. Vizcaíno had been commissioned by the Spanish government to find a calm, protected harbor in Alta California. He named his discovery for the then Viceroy of New Spain, the Conde de Monterrey, and wrote glowingly of its qualities: ". . . we found ourselves to be in the best port that could be desired, for besides being sheltered from all the winds, it has many pines for masts and yards, and live oaks and white oaks, and water in great quantity, all near the shore."[1]

Vizcaíno intended the name Monterey Bay to apply only to the southern part of the bay, near what is now Monterey. Monterey Bay as we know it today, however, has three natural harbors: at Monterey, Santa Cruz, and Capitola. None of these quite live up to Vizcaíno's description since storm waves bombard each at least part of the year. The bay's modest but incomplete protection from fierce Pacific storms played a significant role in the history of Santa Cruz's first lighthouse and in the development of the nearby waterfront.

Although Monterey Bay lost some of its importance when the Spanish discovered San Francisco Bay in 1769, it continued to be an important anchorage. Despite its shortcomings, it is the best natural harbor between San Diego and San Francisco. While under Spanish and Mexican rule, this bay was of additional importance since Monterey served then as the capital of Alta California.

No lighthouses were built in California while under Spain or Mexico, nor was there much need for them. According to Hubert Howe Bancroft's *History of California*, California's non-Indian population in 1845 was only about 7,500. Between 1836 and 1840 only 76 vessels visited California ports. Due to the gold rush, the state's population by mid 1852 had swelled to 255,000. That same year 1,147 vessels arrived at San Francisco.

The first bill passed by the United States Congress appropriating money for lighthouses in California was approved September 28, 1850, only nineteen days after California was admitted to the Union. This bill (for $90,000) and other bills resulted in the construction of sixteen lighthouses on the West Coast during the 1850s: three in Washington Territory, three in Oregon Territory, and ten in California. On June 1, 1854, the first West Coast lighthouse began operation at Alcatraz Island on San Francisco Bay. Point Pinos became the second when lighted February 1, 1855.

In the 1850s and 1860s ships were critical for transporting both goods and people to and from Santa Cruz. Railroads did not arrive here until 1876. Wagon roads, where present, left much to be desired. Following heavy winter rains they were frequently impassable. Because of the geographic isolation created by the heavily forested Santa Cruz Mountains with their deeply incised river valleys, the lumber, lime, leather, and crops produced here were most easily shipped out by boat. A visitor to Santa Cruz in 1852 who worked for the U.S. Coast Survey remarked that this was "the depot of one of the most productive agricultural districts in California."[2] Most certainly a lighthouse was needed to mark the entrance to this port.

In the 1850s California's chief political spokesman in Washington, D.C., was Senator William M. Gwin. Gwin arrived in California from Tennessee in 1849, only a few months before being chosen to later represent California in the U.S. Senate. The senator worked hard for federal legislation, including lighthouses, to benefit the new state. His exact role in securing a lighthouse for Santa Cruz remains uncertain, but he no doubt had a hand in it.

On August 30, 1852, the following was proposed and approved as an amendment to the rather lengthy lighthouse bill then before the U.S. Senate: "For the erection of a light-house at Santa Cruz, California, $30,000."[3] The next day Congress passed the bill and President Millard Fillmore signed it into law.

This very same act of Congress also radically altered the system of administering the nation's lighthouses. It particularly influenced the Pacific Coast lights since none had yet been completed. Earlier, from 1820 to 1852 America's lighthouse system, termed the Lighthouse Establishment, was under the supervision of the Treasury Department's fifth auditor, Stephen Pleasonton. Mr. Pleasonton, whose expertise was in bookkeeping rather than maritime matters, managed to draw considerable criticism during his thirty-two years of service. Although the number of navigational aids increased greatly during this time, their quality did not. The fifth auditor was a bit too thrifty in his management, which on occasion had resulted in lighthouses built of poor quality materials. An investigation ordered by Congress in 1851 revealed that lamps and reflectors in lighthouses were often being inadequately maintained. Mariners were not being properly notified of new navigational aids or changes in old ones. Also, the United States did not have an adequate system for classifying its lighthouses as did England and France. Worst was Pleasonton's reluctance to utilize the Fresnel lens, by then used extensively in Europe to more effectively focus the lights.

Following the exhaustive 1851 investigation, Congress ordered in the 1852 act that the President appoint a nine-member board to manage the nation's system of lighthouses and other navigational aids. The Lighthouse Board was to consist of high ranking army and naval officers as well as military engineers and civilian scientists. They immediately set the highest standards of that time for lighthouse design, construction and maintenance.

Part of the Coast Survey map prepared in 1853 and published in 1854. (Santa Cruz City Museum)

Back in 1848 Congress had ordered the U.S. Coast Survey to begin charting the Pacific Coast. The purpose was to prepare a general map of the entire West Coast of the United States and make more detailed maps of the major harbors showing the water depth, shoreline, and surrounding topography. During the early 1850s the Coast Survey also had the job of examining those West Coast sites for which lighthouses were proposed.

In 1853 Coast Survey Assistant A. M. Harrison led a land party along the northern edge of Monterey Bay. Their assignment was twofold: (1) to prepare a detailed map of the coastline, and (2) to recommend the best site for a lighthouse. Harrison said that if it were deemed desirable to build a lighthouse at Santa Cruz, it should be built at the point labeled "Point Santa Cruz." Harrison described the site in a letter dated December 30, 1853:

> It has as a foundation a substratum of hard rock, covered for several feet with firm earth. It is thirty feet in height, and the light from a lantern forty feet high, placed there, could be seen at a distance of fifteen and two-tenths statute miles from a ship's deck, say ten feet high. The sector of visibility to seaward from this position, exclusive of Monterey bay, would be about 130°; inclusive, 200°.[4]

An 1855 letter reported: "Wood and water are convenient to the site, and bricks of good quality are made in the neighborhood."[5]

Despite the above advantages to erecting a lighthouse at Point Santa Cruz, it was actually not the preferred site of Harrison and his colleagues. The team had also surveyed the coastline at Point Año Nuevo, twenty miles up the coast. Harrison urged in a letter to the superintendent of the Coast Survey, A.D. Bache, that if but one lighthouse were built, it should be located there rather than at Santa Cruz:

> ... it is my opinion that Point Año Nuevo possesses all the

requisites as a site for a guide to Santa Cruz harbor, and would also prove of advantage to vessels in the coasting trade. This point once made, it becomes a matter of little difficulty to reach Santa Cruz; and vessels from the northward, bound to Monterey, and even up and down the coast, would find a light here very serviceable, while one at Point Santa Cruz would avail them but little, if it all.[6]

Lieutenant T. H. Stevens, who had also looked at the two sites, concurred with Harrison. Because a lighthouse at Santa Cruz would serve only local trade, Stevens recommended "the establishment of a light at Año Nuevo as of far greater importance."[7]

The bill passed by Congress, however, was for a lighthouse at Santa Cruz not Point Año Nuevo. A change in that regard would certainly not have been popular with the people of Santa Cruz. Though at that time only a remote community of a few hundred people, Santa Cruz still had more political clout than the scattered whalers and settlers along the coast to the north. Superintendent Bache, who was also a member of the Lighthouse Board, remained neutral on the issue when he forwarded the results of the survey to his boss, Treasury Secretary Guthrie. It is a question, said Bache, "which the Board will probably decide from more general considerations in regard to the lighting of the Western coast than have entered into the views of either of these officers."[8] He therefore abstained from expressing concurrence in their recommendation. In the end, political considerations outweighed the recommendations of the field party and the Lighthouse Board proceeded with plans to build a lighthouse at Point Santa Cruz.

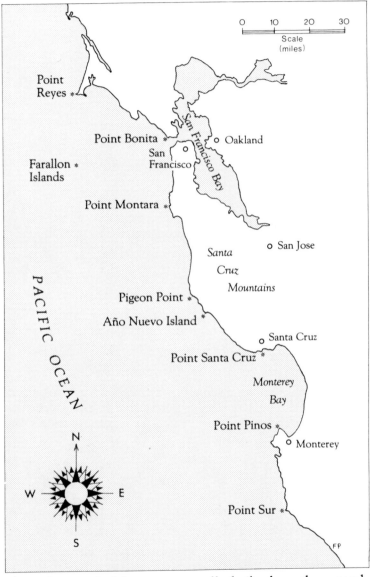

Map showing lighthouses eventually built along the central California coast. A number of lighthouses were also built on San Francisco Bay.

First Attempts Fail

Before the federal government could erect a lighthouse, the site first had to be acquired. This was not always a simple task since all such locations had to be chosen for their navigational merit rather than for their ease of procurement. In the case of the site at Point Reyes, for example, the exorbitant price demanded for the land by its owners forced postponement of lighthouse construction for seventeen years.[9] Tragically, many shipwrecks occurred there during this time which could have been avoided had a warning signal been built earlier. There was also a delay in the construction of a lighthouse at Año Nuevo Island while government officials and land owners dickered over the price for the twenty acres of rock and sand. At Santa Cruz, however, the government faced a different dilemma: no one could figure out who rightfully owned the land.

One of the first people to own the property around Point Santa Cruz was Col. Jonathan D. Stevenson of San Francisco. Colonel Stevenson came to California in March of 1847 in command of a military regiment, the New York Volunteers, to fight against Mexico. Although the Colonel never had the opportunity out West to test his skills in combat, he did prove to be a man of much energy, strong will, and good executive ability. This was later reflected in his real estate adventures.

From 1848, following the war with Mexico but prior to the granting of statehood September 9, 1850, California was a United States territory and was for much of this time under a military government. Through most of this rather chaotic period the previous system of local law, that of Mexico, remained basically in effect. As under Mexico, each district of California was governed by an alcalde, who was a combination judge and administrative officer. He performed the duties of mayor, sheriff, judge, extemporizer of legislation, and presiding officer for the town council if there happened to be one. While California was a United States territory, several different alcaldes were appointed or elected to serve the Santa Cruz District. One of these, Adna A. Hecox, later became Santa Cruz's first lighthouse keeper. Another American alcalde, William Blackburn, granted to various people a considerable amount of land around Santa Cruz. Recipient of a number of lots was none other than Jonathan D. Stevenson. About a dozen men from his former regiment petitioned the Santa Cruz alcalde for lots, most of which were immediately turned over to Stevenson. As a result of this scheme, Stevenson now owned an enormous amount of land in Santa Cruz—nearly a thousand acres in what is now the western part of the town.[10]

The land title situation in California following statehood was a nightmare for many landowners and, more often than not, was a gold mine for lawyers. Besides the alcalde grants, while part of Mexico some 13 million acres of land in California had been granted to individuals by the Mexican government. To evaluate the validity of the Mexican and alcalde grants, Congress in 1851 passed an act creating a Board of Land Commissioners to which each title had to be presented for confirmation or rejection. The rather confusing act, proposed by Senator Gwin, grew to be much criticised over the years for its "guilty until proven innocent" tone. In the case of the Santa Cruz lands, the alcalde grants were not presented to the commissioners for confirmation. This led to Stevenson's eventual undoing, not to mention many years of uneasiness for area residents. As a result of the clouded land title, lighthouse construction was delayed nearly fifteen years.

Lot fifty-eight, the parcel that included Point Santa Cruz, was petitioned for by Stevenson himself on February 28, 1849. The grant was recorded as follows:

William Blackburn, Alcalde of the District of Santa Cruz, grants to J. D. Stevenson, his heirs and assigns forever all of said piece or parcel of land lying in the township of Santa Cruz and bounded on the map of Santa Cruz as follows: on the south and west by the Pacific Ocean and the Bay of Monterey, on the north by lots 55 & 56 and on the east by land owned by George McDougall and the town of Santa Cruz. Said map is now in the office of the Alcalde of Santa Cruz.

Given under my hand and seal this 8th day of March A.D. 1849.

(signed) William Blackburn
Alcalde of the Dist. of Santa Cruz[11]

Over the next several years Stevenson in turn sold parts of this lot to several different people. They, however, apparently did not occupy the land. In 1850, the lot being unfenced and vacant, a Mr. Meridith York decided to take physical possession of it. In 1852 York sold "his" lot to James Cutler for $2,000. Later owners were Alexander McLean, Peter Warner, William Morrow, and Nelson Taylor. All were well known early Santa Cruz citizens except for the original squatter, Mr. York, of whom little else is known.

In the meantime the federal government wanted to build a lighthouse there. The obvious problem was getting clear title to the land. Unlike Morrow, McLean, and the others, the Lighthouse Board was much more particular about such matters. Although the Santa Cruz lighthouse was to be small, it would still be a sizable investment and one that needed to be permanent. From 1854, when the site was selected, through 1858, Major Hartman Bache, inspector for the budding system of West Coast lighthouses, struggled to resolve the problem of the two chains of title. Alas, all efforts failed. Although some of the $30,000 appropriated for a lighthouse at Santa Cruz was spent for the Coast Survey evaluation, most of it ended up being spent elsewhere.

Lighthouse construction ceased in the United States during the Civil War. But soon after the war, continued growth on the West Coast brought a second wave of lighthouse building. In 1865 efforts resumed to procure title to the site selected over a decade earlier at Santa Cruz.

The need for such a navigational aid here continued to grow. More and more of the region's abundant forest, mineral, and agricultural products were being harvested and shipped by coaster to San Francisco and other markets. An extensive system of sawmills was producing lumber and shingles, not to mention staves, barrel heads, fence posts and even telegraph poles. In 1865 Santa Cruz County ranked third in California as a lumber producer and first as a lime producer. Leather, black powder, grain, paper, and tallow were also being produced here in considerable amounts. Two wharves had

Wharves at Santa Cruz, early 1880s. (Vester Dick Photography)

sprouted from the shoreline, ready to feed the holds of waiting schooners and steamers. A small, side-wheel steamer, the *Salinas,* carried passengers regularly between San Francisco and the Monterey Bay area.

Several years prior to the eventual purchase of a lighthouse site, the fact that one had been selected was touted among the attributes of the town. Local citizens realized that a lighthouse would be federal acknowledgment of the importance of Santa Cruz as a seaport. Its construction could even lead to other improvements such as a better harbor.

The renewed effort to erect a lighthouse here meant that Congress would have to pass a new bill appropriating funds. Once again the political cogs began turning. This time it was U.S. Senator Cornelius Cole who pushed for an appropriation. Apparently this was at the urging of William Anthony, Santa Cruz area state assemblyman and a close acquaintance of the senator. Once again merchants and shipping concerns had succeeded in stressing to their political representatives the need for a lighthouse at the north end of Monterey Bay.

On March 2, 1867, Congress again set aside funds for the erection of a lighthouse at Santa Cruz. This time the amount was only $10,000. Since California was much more developed and the Santa Cruz site already surveyed, costs would presumably be less than those projected in 1852. On March 23, 1867, the *Santa Cruz Sentinel* newspaper reported the news:

> We have been shown a letter from the Chief of the Light House Board, endorsed by Senator Cole, to Mr. Wm. Anthony in which it is stated that Santa Cruz is to have a Light House, and also New Year's Point, (where land has been reserved for that purpose). It is suggested "that a breakwater and some defensive works will also be directed at this place." Some improvements will also be made at the mouth of the Salinas River. Senator Cole is making his mark, and will no doubt be one of the most influential and useful Senators . . . .

Almus L. Rountree, who sold the government the lighthouse site. (Santa Cruz County Sheriff's Department)

Again matters were delayed while the title to the site was investigated. Now the owners were Mr. and Mrs. Almus L. Rountree. Mr. Rountree, a native of Tennessee, had at one time worked for the government as a wagonmaster in Arizona and New Mexico. He had come to Santa Cruz County in 1858 and for a while operated a butcher shop on Mission Street and then on Front Street in Santa Cruz. Later, in 1869, he was elected to a two-year term as sheriff and subsequently served as justice of the peace in the nearby town of Felton.

Fortunately for mariners, and for the Rountrees, the land title problems were to finally come to an end. In the late 1850s Jonathan D. Stevenson had filed a lawsuit against those occupying "his" land in Santa Cruz, claiming that they had illegally seized it from him. After losing the suit in the local district court, he appealed to the California Supreme Court. In April of 1868 the court ruled that Stevenson's claim was invalid since it had not been submitted for confirmation to the Board of Land Commissioners in the 1850s.

Mr. and Mrs. Rountree, being aware of the land title problems and anxious to make the sale to the government, obtained the tract in three different ways. First, the bulk of it was purchased from Peter Warner in 1866 for $2,500. Second, they were then granted that same tract by the Trustees of the Town of Santa Cruz (forerunner of the city council) in accordance with an act passed by Congress July 23, 1866. This special act was passed to help rectify the land title situation in Santa Cruz by giving the city authorities the power to simply give title to the present occupants. Third, just to make sure he would have his land no matter what the outcome of the impending court case, Mr. Rountree paid J. D. Stevenson $500 for the tract in July of 1867. Curiously, the parcel had been attached a year earlier for $3,326.73 when Stevenson lost a San Francisco court case.

Following the 1868 California Supreme Court decision, the Lighthouse Board hired the U.S. District Attorney in California to carefully analyze the complex case as it related to the proposed lighthouse site. He pronounced the Rountrees' title valid. His report was later sent to the U.S. Attorney General for examination. The government had good reason to be cautious. At this time the title to the property at the Point Pinos light station was a matter of growing dispute—one that would eventually cost the government $6,000. Finally, in May of 1868 the federal government purchased ten acres of land at Point Santa Cruz for a lighthouse reservation. Actually this was only a small part of the 143-acre tract then owned by the Rountrees. They accepted $2,000 for the parcel, in those days considered a very good deal. Though seemingly a meager sum by today's standards, consider that the entire payment was made in gold coin.

Erecting the Light

The center for the administration of California's lighthouses during the second half of the nineteenth century was the Lighthouse Establishment's Twelfth District office in San Francisco. At the time the Santa Cruz lighthouse was to be built, Lt. Col. Robert S. Williamson, a U.S. Army engineer, was responsible for overseeing the construction and repairing of this district's lighthouses.

On December 14, 1868, Williamson wrote the Lighthouse Board in Washington, D.C., requesting architectural drawings for the lighthouse to be built at Santa Cruz. He did not receive new drawings, but instead was sent plans that had been used to build the Ediz Hook lighthouse, Washington Territory. The Ediz Hook light was built in 1865 on a sandy shoreline protuberance along the Strait of Juan de Fuca, just north of Port Angeles, and was replaced in 1908. Because the plans were reversed when constructing that lighthouse, the Santa Cruz lighthouse was a mirror-image of its twin 750 miles to the north.

The Santa Cruz lighthouse was to be just that—a house with a light on top of it. The plans called for a story-and-a-half dwelling with a square tower on top, all of wood and firmly planted on a brick foundation. On top of the short tower, surrounded by a delicate balustrade, was to rest the small, octagonal room called the lantern. This would house the lens, which would encircle an oil lamp.

In 1869 San Francisco newspapers criticized Lieutenant Colonel Williamson for his handling of certain government transactions, accusing him of favoritism. Soon, he was likewise to alienate Santa Cruz area contractors. He placed the call for bids for the job of building the lighthouse in just one newspaper: the *San Francisco Herald*. Santa Cruz contractors were outraged, noting that the *Herald* was "a democratic organ of limited circulation, and entirely destitute of influence and responsibility."[12] They asked why a notice had not been placed in one of the three newspapers of Santa Cruz County. The lighthouse was, after all, being built here, not seventy miles up the coast. Santa Cruz contractors argued that they could do the work both better and cheaper. The *Santa Cruz Sentinel* newspaper responded by reprinting the notice, but only four days before the 2:00 P.M., June 30, deadline for submission of bids. Unfortunately, apparently no records have survived which list the name of the lighthouse builder.* Silence on the part of local newspapers, however, would seem to indicate it was not a local bidder.

Construction of the lighthouse began in July or early August of 1869. The lantern was made separately at the Lighthouse Establishment's workshop and general depot in Tompkinsville on New York's Staten Island. Lieutenant Colonel Williamson inquired before construction as to the dimensions of the lantern so as to make sure all would fit—a lesson learned the hard way with several of California's earlier lighthouses. On August 31, 1869, he telegraphed Washington, D.C., to report that the building was ready for the lantern and lens. Because the workmen in New York had not yet finished fabricating the lantern, shipment was delayed until early October. In the meantime Williamson examined the lighthouse, approved the work, and paid the builders their fee of $4,350 in gold coin.

*Fires destroyed government records which no doubt listed the name of the builder.

On Wednesday afternoon December 15, 1869, a reporter from the *Santa Cruz Sentinel* visited the lighthouse so as to post his readers on the progress being made:

The painters were at work finishing the cupola, and arranging to set the glass in the lantern. Mr. Oscar Lewis, formerly of Boston, with an assistant, is putting up the lantern and fresnel lens . . . . The lantern is an octagon cast iron frame six feet four inches in diameter with a wrought iron canopy roof. The glass of the lantern is about two by three feet and one fourth of an inch thick—two plates of this glass was [sic] found smashed on opening the boxes, but as spare glasses had been sent no delay was caused . . . . The lamp is not over one inch in diameter, with tubular burner and wick, about the same as a modern parlor lamp; the oil used is best quality winter-strained lard-oil, which is filtered from a reservoir, holding

Santa Cruz lighthouse as it appeared in the early 1880s. (Santa Cruz City Museum)

about half a gallon, immediately above the burner, so as to be kept fluid in cold weather by the heat of the lamp. The fresnel and lamp were manufactured in Paris, France by "L. Sautter & Cie.," for the Lighthouse Board.... The building is elegant and commodious, intended for the keeper's residence, and is divided into six rooms with closets, cellar and a fine store-room. A cistern capable of holding 50,000* gallons of water, other conveniences such as a wood-shed, out-houses, etc. have been built by the Government.... At present, Col. Williamson, the constructing engineer has charge, and the formal possession will not be given until about Christmas or New Year's Eve when the beacon will throw its welcome rays over the broad bay and wide ocean to invite the weary mariner to our harbor, or warn him against the dangers of an iron-bound coast. [13]

A few weeks later the *Santa Cruz County Times* reported:

Mr. A. A. Hecox the newly appointed keeper of the Light House informs us that it will be lighted on Saturday evening Jan. 1st, for the first time. The Government could not have selected a better man than Mr. Hecox for the position. Mr. Hecox will make a diligent and faithful officer and we congratulate him on his appointment. [14]

"May its light always shine, a cheerful beacon to the tempest-tossed mariner," said the *Sentinel* on January 1, 1870. On that day it became the twelfth lighthouse in California to cast its rays upon the Pacific.

As with every lighthouse, the magnificent lens was its most important element. It was expensive too: from $230 to $840 for one the size used at Santa Cruz to over $8,000 for a giant first-order lens. To preserve its gleaming luster, Keeper Hecox cleaned it daily, first brushing it with a feather brush to remove dust, then wiping it with soft linen cloth and polishing it with a buff-skin. When the lens required more rigorous

---

*Government records list the cistern's capacity as 10,000 gallons.

polishing, he applied with a camel's-hair brush a smooth, watery mixture of rouge. When this dried on the glass, he rubbed it off with a buff-skin. During the day he hung blinds to cover the lantern windows so that the lens would not be discolored by prolonged exposure to sunlight.

The type of lens then used in lighthouses was called a Fresnel lens (pronounced frā-něl'), named after Augustin Jean Fresnel of France. He perfected the lens in 1822 utilizing several important discoveries he had made in the study of light and optics. The purpose of this lens, actually a combination of many lenses and prisms, was to make the most efficient use of the rather weak glow of the oil lamps used for illumination at that time. Fresnel cleverly surrounded a lamp with a series of prisms and lenses that gathered the light, which radiated out in all directions, and focused it to a single, horizontal plane. This increased the intensity of the light many-fold when viewed from the proper position.

The Santa Cruz lighthouse's fifth-order lens, second from the smallest size made, stood 19 inches high and had an inside diameter of 14½ inches. It was composed of 15 lens elements and 36 prisms, all made of hand-polished flint glass and set in a brass framework. This was certainly a far cry from the first-order lenses, which measured nearly eight feet high, weighed several thousand pounds, and were composed of over one thousand separate lens elements. Small Fresnel lenses were typically used for bay and harbor lights. First-order lenses were installed at major lighthouses on the open coast such as at Point Sur, Pigeon Point and Point Reyes where more powerful beams were needed.

Thanks to Augustin Fresnel, France had a virtual monopoly on the manufacturing of lighthouse lenses during the nineteenth century. At one time three different Paris optical companies manufactured the lenses: Barbier & Fenestre; Sautter, Lemonnier et Cie; and Henry Lepaute. The French government

NOTICE TO MARINERS.

(**No. 99.**)

UNITED STATES OF AMERICA—CALIFORNIA.

Light-House at the entrance to the Harbor of Santa Cruz, California.

Notice is hereby given that on and after the 1st day of January, 1870, a harbor light will be exhibited on the Light-house recently erected at the entrance to the harbor of Santa Cruz. California, at a point called Point Santa Cruz.

The illuminating apparatus is of the fifth order of Fresnel, showing a *fixed white* light through an angle of 270°.

The light is elevated 69 feet above mean sea-level, and should be seen from the deck of a sea going vessel. in clear weather, 14 nautical miles. The lantern and lens are on a small wooden tower on the keeper's dwelling.

The tower and lantern are painted white; dome of lantern painted red.

The keeper's dwelling is a one and one-half story frame building, painted white, with green blinds to the windows. Out houses are painted white.

The main structure is 300 feet from the extremity of the bluff point. The distance from base to focal plane is 35½ feet; the distance from mean sea-level to base 33½ feet. A vessel coming from the northward can first see the light when it bears E. ¾ N.

The Light-house is in latitude 36° 57' 00" north; longitude 122° 00' 32" west.

The magnetic variation at the place is 15° 45' E.

Bearings and distances to prominent objects:

Light-house at Point Pinos S.E. by S. ½ S. 19¾ nautical miles.

Point Sauquil E. by N. ¾ N. 2½ nautical miles.

By ORDER OF THE LIGHT-HOUSE BOARD,

W. B. SHUBRICK,
Chairman.

TREASURY DEPARTMENT,

OFFICE LIGHT-HOUSE BOARD,

Washington, D. C., December 28, 1869.

regulated each and decided what prices they could charge.[15]

Under the Lighthouse Board an elaborate system was devised for classifying lighthouses and parts of lighthouses. Inside the fifth-order lens used at Santa Cruz was a fifth-order Funck's Hydraulic Float Lamp (fourth-, fifth-, and sixth-order lamps looked about the same). All this was housed in a fourth-order lantern (commonly used for fourth-, fifth- and sixth-order lenses) which sat atop a sixth-order building.

The Santa Cruz light was originally a fixed white light, glowing steadily each night from sunset to sunrise from a height sixty-nine feet above mean sea level. In 1880, under orders from the Lighthouse Board, Keeper Hecox replaced the lamp's clear glass chimney with one tinted red, thus producing a fixed red light. This change in the light's characteristics enabled seamen to better distinguish it from other lighthouses along the central California coast, particularly from the Point Pinos lighthouse. According to the Lighthouse Board's 1890 *Light List*, the sequence was as follows: Point Sur, flashing red and white; Point Pinos, fixed white; Point Santa Cruz, fixed red; and Pigeon Point, flashing white. Those that flashed could be further distinguished by differing times between flashes. In 1890 the Pigeon Point light flashed once every ten seconds, whereas the Farallon Island light, which was also white, flashed only once each minute.

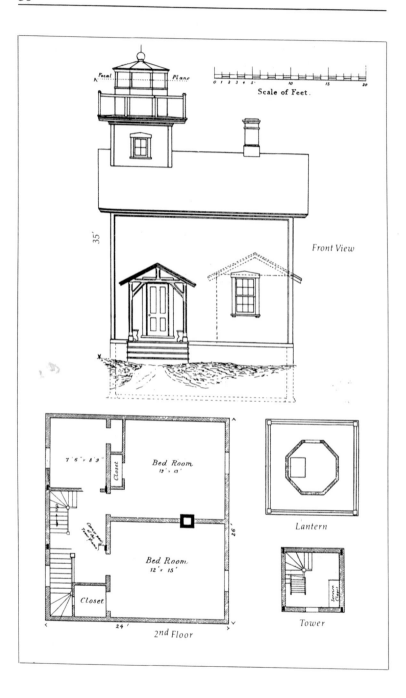

Focal Plane

Scale of Feet.

35′

Front View

7′6″ × 8′9″

Closet

Bed Room
12′ × 13′

Closet

Bed Room
12′ × 15′

24′

26′

2nd Floor

Lantern

Tower

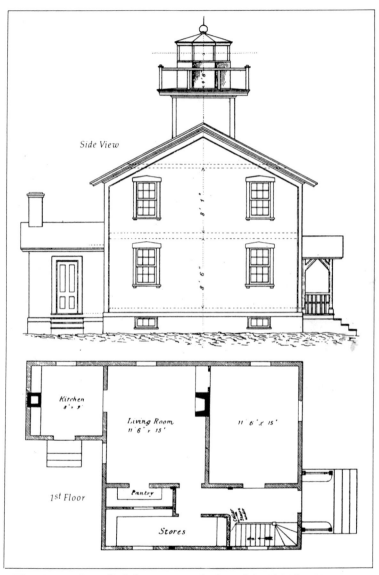

The Santa Cruz lighthouse was designed in 1864 by Hartman Bache, former lighthouse inspector and cousin of Coast Survey Superintendent A.D. Bache (*Manual of Lighthouse Engineering*, Government Printing Office: 1869)

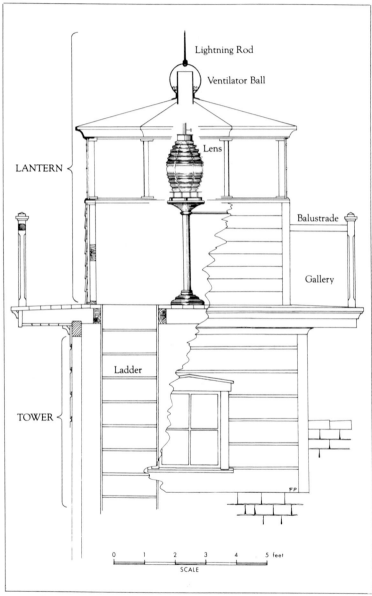

Cross section of lighthouse lantern and tower, showing lens.
(Modified from various sources)

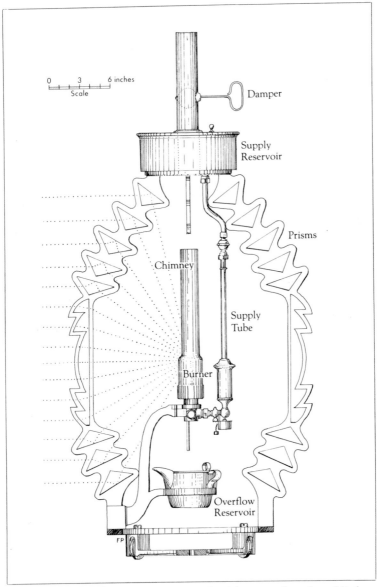

Cross section of lens showing lard oil lamp and paths of light rays. (Modified from *Manual of Lighthouse Engineering*, Government Printing Office: 1869)

Mariner's view of the Santa Cruz lighthouse, early 1880s. (Santa Cruz City Museum)

Pioneer Family Finds Home Watching Over Bay

The original Santa Cruz lighthouse was built to be more or less a one-person operation and remained so throughout its existence. Amazingly, only three different individuals served there as keepers during its seventy-one years of operation. This was partly due to fate and partly due to the desirability of the station as a home. The first keeper of the lighthouse, Adna A. Hecox, came with his family to California overland from Illinois in 1846, the same year the famous Donner party was trapped by a Sierra blizzard while attempting a similar journey.

Adna Hecox was born in 1806 at Grosse Ile near Detroit, Michigan. At the age of six, the War of 1812 ravaged his homeland, forcing his family to flee to Detroit. In 1829 he married his first wife, who died of cholera in 1834. In 1836 he married nineteen-year-old Margaret M. Hamer of Pennsylvania and eventually settled with her on a thirty-acre farm in Illinois. He later worked as a carpenter and lead miner but frequently suffered from poor health, particularly during the icy winters. After reading some pamphlets distributed by John Bidwell about the mild climate and rich farmland in California, Hecox grew eager to move there. His wife shuddered at the thought of such a long journey to a foreign land. She was convinced that they would all end up dead along some trail through the distant wilderness.

On March 23, 1846, the fifth birthday of their daughter Catherine, the Hecox family set out for California. Their daughter Sara was seven; Ellen was three; and tiny Adna H.

Hecox was not quite one. The family eventually joined a party led by Charles Imus and Joseph Aram.

At that time California was still part of Mexico. However, it seemed certain that there would soon be war between the United States and Mexico, and that under those circumstances the United States would seize California.

After the members of the party crossed the Mississippi River, they were drenched by heavy rains. For days their covered wagons splashed through the mud and slush. Their only consolation at that point was the abundant wild turkeys which were quite plump and proved to be most tasty roasted over an open fire. On May 10, two days after ferrying across the Missouri River, the members left behind what was to their eyes the last traces of civilization.

Though Mrs. Hecox found little to smile about along the ensuing trek, few could question her courage or stamina. The party had to make its own roads, often following Indian or bison trails. Mr. Hecox took ill on many occasions, leaving his wife to drive the wagon as well as tend to the children, fix the meals, and keep things in at least a modest state of tidiness. One evening, while preparing supper, a huge swarm of inch-long black beetles descended upon the entire camp. "You can't imagine how dreadful they were," recalled Mrs. Hecox. "The air was literally full of them."[16] Dozens of the hard-shelled creatures clung to the hair and clothes of her frightened daughters. The pan in which she was frying some meat was full in an instant. After Mrs. Hecox cleared the wagon of the repulsive insects as best she could, she and the children shut themselves inside the wagon while the men desperately tried to keep the livestock from stampeding. "I never heard men swear so dreadfully," she said. "We passed a wretched night, and it was days before we were entirely rid of the bugs, though there seemed to be but that one swarm . . . . "[17]

On the first of October the members of the party emerged

Adna A. Hecox, keeper of the Santa Cruz lighthouse from 1870 to 1883. (Courtesy Stan Stevens)

from the Sierra and camped for the first time in the Sacramento Valley. *This* was beautiful California? The dry, dusty valley, parched by the summer's heat, brought disappointment beyond words, especially for Mrs. Hecox. After looking about for a while she simply crawled into her wagon and cried. To add to her misery, the next day Captain Swift from Sutter's Fort came to their camp to ask the men to join Frémont's battalion to fight against Mexico.

The Hecox family immediately sought safety at the somewhat dilapidated Mission Santa Clara with other recent immigrants while skirmishes between the Americans and Mexican authorities continued. Lacking food, clean water, and medical attention, a number of the immigrants died that winter at the mission. Mr. Hecox suffered from typhoid, but amazingly all of his family survived the damp, dark quarters. Not until after a battle about ten miles from Santa Clara near the end of the war did the immigrants finally feel it was safe to leave the old mission. Many, including Mrs. Hecox, had stood guard there, fearing that they might be fired upon by Mexican soldiers.

On February 20, 1847, the Hecox family eagerly left Mission Santa Clara, traveling by ox team to Gilroy and then through the Pajaro Valley to Soquel. Because it was raining and there were no roads, they once again sloshed through mud most of the way. Mrs. Hecox described their journey and arrival in Soquel after eight days:

> From the ranches we passed, the Spanish women came to us and gave us milk, cheese, and sugar. Some of our company were afraid to eat the things they were given, fearing they had been poisoned, on account of the bad feelings existing in the country; but father [Mr. Hecox] and I were not afraid, and we never had reason to regret our confidence. After we left San Juan, the Spaniards told us to kill a beef wherever we might happen to find one. We were to hang the skin on the limb of a tree, that they might know by the brand to whom it belonged. We took them at their word, and killed two on our trip.
>
> After we arrived at Soquel we camped for about a week, and then moved into a shanty we found unoccupied. This was in a lovely place near the Soquel Creek, and from the day we entered the weather was heavenly. It was so warm and clear, the air was so pure and the new grass so fresh and green, that father [Mr. Hecox], though he was not yet well, was perfectly enraptured. He went about rubbing his hands and asking me if I wasn't glad *now* that I had come to California. It did seem wonderful, the perfect spring, while according to our reckoning it should still be winter, or at any rate cold and blustering.[18]

In those days, there being no stores in Soquel or at nearby Santa Cruz, goods had to be brought all the way from Monterey. "Soquel is not the same place now that it was then," she said forty-five years later in an 1892 *Overland Monthly* article. "Of course the climate remains, but the beauty of the place has been destroyed by civilization."[19]

Margaret M. Hecox, wife of the first keeper. (Courtesy Stan Stevens)

Shortly after the Hecox family arrived in Soquel Mr. Hecox, with the help of several others, built a sawmill on Soquel Creek for an Irishman named Michael Lodge. Lodge's wife, Martina Castro, had been granted ranchos Soquel and Soquel Augmentation by the Mexican government. These totaled over 34,000 acres, most of it heavily forested.

Like many of the early American settlers, Hecox laid claim to several firsts. During the summer of 1847 he built a billiard table, the first in California. It was made of redwood and later used in Monterey. Some historians also credit him with having preached the first Protestant sermon in California. More likely, this distinction belonged to the chaplain of the Francis Drake expedition. Hecox was a licensed minister of the Methodist Episcopal Church and was also a strong temperance advocate. According to his wife, he had learned from bitter experience in his younger days the curse of drunkenness and wished to raise his children in a sober community. He helped establish the first Methodist Church in Santa Cruz as well as several temperance societies.

Early in 1848 word of James Marshall's gold discovery reached Hecox and the others working at the Soquel mill. The men left quickly for the Sierra foothills, desperately hoping for a rich strike. Hecox left too, after first settling his family in slightly better quarters at Santa Cruz. Adna Hecox was gone four months and was among the men who discovered the diggings at Hangtown, now called Placerville. On one day he and two partners are said to have picked up six pounds of gold. Too bad their luck ran out. In the long run the venture barely paid for itself. In fact, the men would have made more money at the mill. Later that year Mr. Hecox returned to the mines with Joseph Aram, this time to sell goods to the miners. This proved to be more profitable.

Soon after returning to Santa Cruz permanently, Hecox launched his career in local politics. In the fall of 1849, while California was a United States territory, he was elected alcalde of the Santa Cruz District and apparently remained in office until statehood. As alcalde, his name headed a petition of 142 signatures presented to the California Senate in San Jose on January 16, 1850, requesting that Santa Cruz be made a separate county from Monterey County. During the two decades following statehood, Hecox, a Republican, held numerous local government offices including justice of the peace, public administrator, treasurer, and judge.

In October of 1869 the federal government began accepting applications for the upcoming lightkeeper's position at Santa Cruz. There was no shortage of applicants, nor was there a shortage of people willing to endorse those who applied. Some of the lists of signatures were a yard long! Hecox's many skills, brief military service during the war with Mexico, and political endorsements no doubt helped him get the job. He was nominated for the position December 13, 1869, by J. F. Miller of San Francisco who, as collector of customs, was also superintendent of the lights.

Santa Cruz lighthouse, circa 1887. The lantern was painted black shortly after this photo was taken. (National Archives)

The job of lighthouse keeping, though often romanticized, was most often described by the keepers themselves as monotonous. Every day the lamp had to be cleaned, the lens dusted, the wicks trimmed. The latter duty earned keepers the nickname "wickies."

Adna Hecox, though the only paid keeper at Santa Cruz, was not alone in tending the light. Family participation was common practice in lighthouses and encouraged by the Lighthouse Board as a way to keep the families living together, not to mention the saving of salaries for additional keepers. The job of trimming the wicks, for example, belonged to Hecox's youngest daughter, Laura.

Lighthouse keepers were supposed to meet several requirements for the job. They had to be able to read and write, keep accurate accounts, do the required manual labor, and sail a boat. Also, they needed to have enough mechanical ability to keep the light and premises in good order. Two violations in particular would bring swift dismissal. If a keeper was found intoxicated, he would not only be dismissed but ejected immediately from the station. Obviously this was unlikely in the case of Keeper Hecox. Also, allowing the light to fail was unforgivable. The Lighthouse Board considered it the duty of every keeper to stand by his light as long as the lighthouse stood. "For him to desert it when in danger is as cowardly as for a soldier to leave his guns on the advance of an enemy," warned the board.[20] More than once in United States history keepers literally went down with their lighthouses.

Santa Cruz was without doubt one of the most pleasant and least dangerous light stations at which to work. Tucked under Monterey Bay's gently-curving northern rim, the weather was, for the most part, mild. Within easy walking distance of downtown Santa Cruz, it contrasted drastically with the island stations to the north such as the Southeast Farallon and Año Nuevo. There, weeks could roll by before keepers would see another human being. The Hecoxes kept chickens, a cow, a horse, and, in the northwest corner of the reservation, a 150-by-270-foot vegetable garden. In a 1907 report, the keeper said conditions there were "considered very healthful."[21] It was a peaceful life, the salty air punctuated by the squawking gulls, the barking sea lions, and the gentle ocean roar.

Shipwreck!

Seldom did events interrupt the tranquillity at Lighthouse Point. One surprise, however, awaited the Hecox family when they awoke on the morning of October 26, 1876. A schooner, loaded with 3,000 railroad ties, sat hopelessly mired in the wet sand of the beach below the lighthouse. Named the *Active*, she had a seven-man crew and was from San Francisco. When the wind died that night, the ship dropped both anchors while off Lighthouse Point. Unfortunately, a strong swell soon developed, powered by some distant storm. Lacking sufficient breeze to set sail, the schooner was now at nature's mercy. The heavy swells drove the ship onto the beach at four o'clock that morning. None of the crew was injured, but the ship's rudder, keel, and stern post were destroyed. Though at first it was thought that the vessel could be saved, the $19,000 ship ended up a loss. She had only been insured for $3,000. Laura Hecox, who was an avid collector of just about everything, kept for many years some souvenirs from the *Active* including a skylight presented to her by the captain.

Lighthouse Point, being set back from the open coast, was hardly a threat to ships. This was the only shipwreck in its history. In fact, the lighthouse there was classified as a harbor light, intended to guide ships to the port of Santa Cruz rather than warn them of any great danger. The *Active* got caught outside Santa Cruz's natural harbor. But even had she dropped anchor inside the harbor, she would not have been entirely protected from heavy swells.

The problem with Santa Cruz's natural harbor is (and was)

Wreck of the schooner *Active*. (Santa Cruz City Museum)

simple. Although the shallow, sandy-bottomed embayment between Point Santa Cruz and Soquel Point provides good shelter in northerly weather, northwest winds frequently create large waves which sweep around the point, past the lighthouse, and into the bay. The harbor grants no refuge at all from southerly winds when, as summed up bluntly in an old *Pacific Coast Pilot*, "vessels are obliged to leave."

Through the years countless boats have been driven onto the northern Monterey Bay shoreline by southerly swells. The month of October has become particularly notorious, and modern-day seafarers would do well to heed the past. Arthur Anderson, keeper of the Santa Cruz lighthouse from 1916 to 1940 said that the highest surf he ever saw there was during the month of October in 1940. There was the beaching of a naval submarine called the *F-1* (October 12, 1912), the wreck of the steamer *La Feliz* (October 1, 1924), and the luxury yacht *Shamrock VI* (October 7, 1972). In October of 1979, giant swells wrenched seventeen boats from their moorings off Capitola, most of them never to be seen again.

In 1867 when money was appropriated for a lighthouse at Santa Cruz, plans were already in the works to improve the harbor over which the lighthouse would soon stand guard. Generally agreed upon as the best solution was a giant breakwater. Such a stone barrier could extend from Lighthouse Point nearly a mile into Monterey Bay yet only be in forty feet of water. It would not only help keep ships from being driven ashore by heavy storm waves, but also protect the wharves from storm damage. Calmer waters would also facilitate the transfer of cargo.

Shortly after the lighting of the Santa Cruz lighthouse, several studies were conducted to determine the feasibility and desirability of erecting a breakwater eastward into northern Monterey Bay from Lighthouse Point. The last of these early investigations, completed in 1873 by Lt. Col. C. S. Stewart, a U.S. Army engineer, was far from favorable. The plan called for a breakwater 2,300 yards long at an estimated cost of over 10 million dollars. Stewart felt that the tremendous cost clearly outweighed its possible benefit to commerce. He also warned that the project could take decades to complete.

But the breakwater idea was not sunk completely. In the

1890s it surfaced again. "A breakwater secured and we will have the world," said the *Sentinel*. "A little city will spring into a great city, and the repose of the rest-hunters will be disturbed by rattle of thousands of factory wheels. Then Santa Cruz will be the terminus of inland railroads, ship and car coming together and transferring their burdens without breaking freight."[22] It was the railroads, however, which eliminated the need for a better harbor by taking over the transporting of goods from this area. Federal studies once again proved negative, also citing Santa Cruz's proximity to the existing port of San Francisco. Many more harbor proposals were to come and go before Wood's Lagoon was finally dredged in the early 1960s to create the present Santa Cruz Small Craft Harbor.

On October 1, 1924, strong swells drove the *La Feliz* ashore two miles west of the Santa Cruz lighthouse.

Caves Endanger Lighthouse

The Lighthouse Board was very careful about selecting sites for lighthouses. Though each site had to be carefully surveyed beforehand, errors in judgment were inevitable. Both the Point Bonita and Point Loma lighthouses, for example, had eventually to be rebuilt. Their original high elevations, though enabling their light beams to be seen for great distances when clear, caused them often to be shrouded by fog. West Coast fogs, it was learned, frequently were only at this higher level, making visibility much greater nearer the water.

At Santa Cruz the lighthouse became a pawn in a more rigorous battle against the elements. In late 1878 Lt. Col. R. S. Williamson, still engineer for the Twelfth Lighthouse District, returned to Santa Cruz to examine the increasingly precarious situation. What he found, to his dismay, was a lighthouse being undermined by three sea caves, each carved over the years by the erosive action of the ocean waves.

On the southeast side of the point were two caves: one eighty-three feet long, fifty feet wide, and sixteen feet high at the mouth; the other ninety feet long, sixty-five feet wide, and twenty-five feet high at the mouth. Directly west of the lighthouse, penetrating the side of the point, was a third cave, slightly smaller. The largest cave extended back to within twelve feet of the corner of the lighthouse. Should the southeast caves collapse, say during a storm, much of the Hecox's front yard would tumble into the resulting thirty-foot chasm. On December 9, 1878, Williamson wrote to the Lighthouse

Board describing his cave explorations. A more detailed report, filed in mid February of 1879, brought prompt orders: relocate the lighthouse.

Had the lighthouse been built out of brick or stone, the entire situation would have been much more costly, not to mention embarrassing. Congress would have had to appropriate funds for a new lighthouse. Fortunately, the Santa Cruz lighthouse was a sturdy, wood-frame structure and, in the next several weeks, was simply jacked up, placed on wooden rollers, and pulled back about three hundred feet using teams of horses or oxen. A new foundation and cistern had to be built, the originals being of brick and therefore quite immovable. The lighthouse also benefited from the first of several enlargements. The small room at the back, which contained the kitchen, was extended to the full width of the building.

It turned out that the caves did not collapse suddenly as had been feared. Nevertheless, if the old lighthouse was in existence today, and on the original site, a sizable part of it would be dangling over the cliff. The cliff above the southeast caves gradually eroded and collapsed at a rate of about a foot per year to form a small cove.

Ironically, part of this history repeated itself in recent years as the sea caves that threatened the lighthouse a century earlier drew concern once again. The single descendent of the southeast caves still exists, undercutting the back of the cove. In late 1978, almost exactly a hundred years after Lieutenant Colonel Williamson recognized the danger of the situation, the city of Santa Cruz applied to the California Coastal Commission for a permit to plug the cave. The reason given was public safety and, ultimately, the threat to the present brick lighthouse which was built, perhaps unwisely, nearly two hundred feet seaward of the site to which the original lighthouse was moved. Environmental concerns

Plugging the sea cave in November, 1980.

forced modification and postponement of the project until October and November of 1980 when the forty-foot cave was plugged with reinforced concrete.

The most spectacular geologic feature of Lighthouse Point's past was the giant rock arch that graced the point's east side opposite the relocated lighthouse. This picturesque bit of nature's handywork spanned some thirty feet and rose nearly twenty feet. Low tides created a beach beneath it—a secluded spot where Laura Hecox liked to hunt for unusual sea creatures. As the tide came in, the water swirled and sloshed below it, giving life to the barnacles and limpets that clung to its base. The precarious sandstone bridge supported many a daring pedestrian in its heyday, much to the delight of tourists. In December of 1888, however, the ocean which had given it birth finally brought its demise. The *Daily Surf,* rival newspaper of the *Santa Cruz Sentinel,* mirrored the community's

Natural arch on the east side of Lighthouse Point, 1888. (Vester Dick Photography)

View from same location as above, 1981.

sadness over the fallen landmark, yet offered some optimism as well as a poke at the competition:

> Pilgrims and pedestrians to the ruins of the arch . . . have been numerous since this fine clear weather has usurped the rain storm which did the damage. It is rather a mournful sight to see the pile of sandstone *debris* which lies at the foot of the cliff, and the tall column of sandstone which stands mateless, looks lonely with only the sea gulls flying around its summit. It stands like a sentinel but it, too, is rapidly wearing away— the *"Sentinel"* is being slowly destroyed by the "Surf"—said a bright observer; its fate is certainly assured.
>
> The next point adjoining is preparing for popularity also. A low arch is already formed, at least ten feet above the water at its highest point. Through this the waves are dashing constantly and with all the force of a giant sculptor they are preparing for generations yet to come another arch, perhaps even more artistic and graceful than the one we have just lost.[23]

The old lighthouse reservation shrunk a little through the decades as the waves etched its cliffs inch by inch. In 1868 the property line was mapped extending across the natural arch, it undoubtedly having been more substantial then. Several times, fences and roadways had to be moved back due to eroding cliffs. In 1901 a granite monument marking a corner of the reservation likewise had to be moved as waves were washing away the ground around it. In the 1930s those who again pushed for construction of a breakwater at Lighthouse Point argued that it would not only create a better harbor but also slow cliff erosion north of the lighthouse. This "improvement," however, quite likely would have robbed sand from beaches further down the coast, thus worsening erosion problems elsewhere.

Keeper Laura Hecox and her mother on the front steps of the Santa Cruz lighthouse, 1888. (Santa Cruz City Museum)

Keeper's Daughter "Inherits" Post

On Saturday, March 17, 1883, the flag at the Santa Cruz lighthouse was lowered to half-mast. Adna Hecox had "breathed his last," reported the local newspaper. The death at the lighthouse of the seventy-seven-year-old pioneer was not unexpected. He had been ill for quite some time, during which his daughter, Laura, had increasingly assumed the duties of caring for the light. After her father's death, her brother-in-law, Captain Albert Brown of San Francisco, personally recommended to federal officials there that Miss Hecox be appointed keeper. Within a week she was formally assigned this duty.

In his will Adna Hecox left to each of his children ten dollars. His wife inherited the rest of the estate, the most valuable being two pieces of land on the southeast corner of Mission and Rigg streets in Santa Cruz. They had occupied one of these prior to moving into the lighthouse. Also left to her were various personal effects, two notes for a total of $280 against Mr. A. Brown, two dozen chickens, one chest of carpenter's tools, one horse with harness, one cow, assorted farm equipment, and "a lot of old lumber."

Laura Hecox stayed on as lighthouse keeper for thirty-three years, not once allowing the light to fail. Women lightkeepers were not uncommon in late nineteenth century America. Noted lighthouse historian Francis Ross Holland, Jr., in his book *America's Lighthouses,* ventured that probably almost all United States lighthouses whose histories go back at least to the 1800s at one time or another had female assistant keepers.

A surprising number had women as principal keepers. Across Monterey Bay, at Point Pinos, there were two. Mrs. Charlotte Layton was appointed head keeper in 1856 after her husband, the first keeper, was killed in a chase after an outlaw as part of a sheriff's posse. In 1893 Mrs. Emily A. Fish was appointed keeper there. Her nephew, Henry Nichols, was inspector for this lighthouse district, and her husband, a Civil War veteran, was recently deceased.[24] Provided they were capable of the work, the Lighthouse Board gave preference to those women who wished to succeed their husbands or fathers as keepers. An official government list in 1894 showed that Miss Hecox and Mrs. Fish were among twenty women at that time who served as keepers at various lighthouses around the nation.

From childhood, Laura Hecox had a keen interest in the natural world around her. After moving into the lighthouse with her parents, she spent countless hours exploring the nearby beaches and tidepools. A true nature lover and a compulsive collector, she assembled through the many years an impressive collection of shells, minerals, Indian artifacts, fossils, and other curios.

Laura Hecox was not the only nineteenth century lighthouse resident to take up collecting as a hobby. The daughter of one of the keepers at Point Montara, just south of San Francisco, displayed to visitors her large collection of "marine curiosities." Sea shells were also the specialty of Mrs. Mary Israel, who for three years was assistant keeper at the Point Loma lighthouse, San Diego.

Miss Hecox was tied to Santa Cruz both by her love of the place and the nightly ritual of keeping the light. Perhaps this is why she delighted in gathering curios from near and far to share with both visitors and residents of this seaside community. Eventually Miss Hecox turned the front room of the lighthouse into a small museum. She exhibited her collec-

Mrs. Margaret Hecox with friends in front of lighthouse, 1887. (Santa Cruz City Museum)

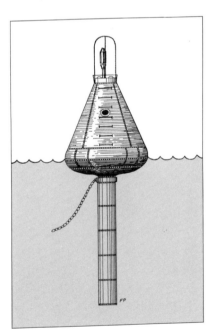

A whistling buoy such as this was anchored off Lighthouse Point by the federal government in 1888 to further aid mariners. Its compressed-air whistle was powered by wave action. The rise and fall of the water drew air into a cylinder and forced it out through the whistle.

tions in upright glass-fronted cabinets that had been built for her out of cherrywood by her father. Besides samples of the local fauna and flora, she also displayed beautifully-carved Eskimo artifacts; and clubs, spears, and other implements made by the inhabitants of south sea islands. One case was filled with sea shells and corals from the tropics. Beside the front porch rested several giant bones from a whale. All this made a visit to the Santa Cruz lighthouse far from ordinary.

Tourists visiting the main beach at Santa Cruz found the lighthouse, visible in the distance, an irresistible attraction. As keeper, it was part of Miss Hecox's duty to open the station regularly to public inspection. A sign at the entrance to the reservation indicated the days and hours during which visitors would be received. When the weather was good, there was a steady stream of lighthouse visitors.

A writer visiting in 1904 described the keeper as a most pleasant little woman, standing guard at the front door, armed with a big feather duster. Everywhere inside the lighthouse, everything was spotless and speckless. To keep it that way, Miss Hecox often gave visitors' apparel a deft whisking before admitting them inside. She then presented the pen for signing the guest register. The book listed visitors from China, Japan, Europe, and nearly every state in the Union.

The tour began with a climb up several flights of stairs to the watchroom, so named because this was where the keeper often stood watch over the light above. Next, one climbed nearly vertically through a trapdoor into the octagonal lantern room where Miss Hecox stood waiting. On a post in the center of the tiny room stood the magnificent lens. "You won't touch it, will you, please?" were her first words. The keeper smiled as she cautioned each visitor, yet the tone of her voice was said to have bespoke the weight of her responsibility.

Although Miss Hecox told countless visitors how the powerful light was produced, a spark of enthusiasm always punctuated her sentences. For each group of visitors crammed into the lantern, she opened the door on the side of the lens and placed her hand inside the lens to demonstrate its great magnifying power. A genuine light of love was said to show in her eyes as she gazed at the lens and oil lamp that she and her father had cared for through the many years.

Miss Hecox began her daily chore at sunrise when she slowly lowered the flame and gently blew across the top of the chimney to extinguish the light. She then hung the curtains to the lantern windows and began cleaning the lens, chimney, and the glass panes of the lantern. Before lighting at sunset she filled two lamps with oil. After placing one of the lamps inside the lens, she lighted the wick, keeping the flame low at first so as to avoid cracking the glass chimney

Keeper Laura Hecox cleaning the kerosene lamp used each night as the lighthouse's illuminating source. (Santa Cruz City Museum)

by heating it too fast. Because the lamp did not hold enough oil to burn properly all night, at midnight she lit the second lamp and exchanged it with the first. Since Miss Hecox did not have a paid assistant, she was not required to watch the light continuously except when it was stormy. During calm weather she usually checked the light twice each night.

By 1890, most lighthouses that had been using lard oil as fuel for their lamps had been converted to kerosene. The primary reason for the change was economy. By 1889 lard oil had risen in cost to 57 cents per gallon while kerosene, or "mineral oil" as it was then called, cost only 8½ cents per gallon.[25] The changeover had been slow since lamps that would burn the new substance had to be built and installed in each lighthouse. Also, new containers had to be manufactured to store and transport the oil because of its more volatile and explosive nature. The smaller lights, such as the

Oil house. (U.S. Coast Guard)

one at Santa Cruz, were the first to burn the new fuel, the switch occurring in the late 1870s.

The use of kerosene soon brought concern about storage of this fuel within lighthouses. The safest place to store the extra supplies of this dangerous liquid would be in separate buildings well away from dwellings and lights. The Lighthouse Board, in its 1890 annual report, urged Congress to appropriate money for special oil houses:

> As the quantity of the oil now used is larger, and as its bulk is greater than was that of the oil formerly used, and as the mineral oil is much more likely to occasion fire, and indeed to take fire, than was the lard oil, the Board has come to the conclusion, in the interest of safety, to advise that the proper steps be taken to have a house erected at each of the larger stations from a plan specially devised after careful study for the purpose.

Congress, however, was slow to respond. The Santa Cruz light station did not get an oil house until 1907. The tiny concrete structure, about five by eight feet, was built seventy-five feet west of the lighthouse. It was lined with wooden shelves capable of holding 120 five-gallon cans of oil—a year's supply.

In all, the Hecox family kept the Santa Cruz beacon shining for forty-six years. Although Miss Hecox was quick to remind visitors that this was Uncle Sam's lighthouse, it must have been hard for her to keep from feeling at least a little as though the place was hers. She lived there from age fifteen until she retired at age sixty-two. Three members of the Hecox family died there, and three couples were married there. Mrs. Margaret Hecox resided at the lighthouse until her death in 1908 at age ninety-three. In later years one of Laura Hecox's brothers, Adna H. Hecox, also resided at the lighthouse as did one of her sisters, Alwilda Organ, and Mrs. Organ's husband, Rev. Thomas Organ.

It was Mrs. Organ who happened to be standing on the stairway below the light when the terrible earthquake of 1906 struck. The lighthouse's massive timbers, though they creaked and groaned, refused to give in to this, their greatest test. The glass chimney of the lamp, however, was shattered into a myriad of tiny pieces. Only the quick action of Miss Hecox kept the light burning.

Throughout her career as lightkeeper, Laura Hecox earned $750 per year—average pay for many jobs at that time. Added to this, of course, was the benefit of a place to live. Unfortunately, Congress did not pass a bill appropriating money for keepers' pensions until 1918—two years after Miss Hecox retired and moved to a tiny cottage at the Advent Christian Campground, two miles east of town. She died there in 1919.

By 1904 the cypress trees around the lighthouse had grown considerably.

No. 4

TO VISITORS.

Visitors will be courteously and politely received, and admitted into the Tower and Lantern, except as specified below. The *Light Keeper*, or the *Assistant Keeper*, on duty is responsible for any *injury* or *defacement* to the *Buildings, Lenses, Lamps, Glazing of the Lantern*, and to any other *Property* belonging to the *Light Station* under his charge. unless he can identify parties who may have done the injury, so as to make *them* accountable for it; and any such damage will be reported immediately to the Inspector or Engineer of the District, with the names of the person or persons, if they can be ascertained.

It is therefore requested that persons who visit this Light Station will be careful not to handle or touch the *Illuminating Apparatus*, scratch or deface the plate glass of the Lantern, cut the woodwork, or write upon the window glass or painted or whitewashed parts of the Buildings, or do any other injury to the premises.

No person not connected with the Light Station will be allowed in the Watch room or Lantern between sunset and sunrise.

By order of the Lighthouse Board:

FRANCIS J. HIGGINSON,

Rear Admiral, U. S. N., Chairman.

Thomas Perry,

Captain, U. S. N., Naval Secretary.

R. L. Hoxie,

Major, Corps of Engineers, U. S. A., Engineer Secretary.

TREASURY DEPARTMENT,

Office Lighthouse Board, Washington, D. C., August 31, 1899.

Notice to lighthouse visitors, dated 1899. (Pacific Grove Museum)

This 1940 view shows the many additions built onto the lighthouse in later years. (Vester Dick Photography)

Twilight of an Era

In 1909 and 1910 the Lighthouse Board had big plans for the Santa Cruz lighthouse: install a fourth-order lens (a size larger than the one being used), erect a steam-powered fog signal to augment the existing offshore whistling buoy, and construct dwellings for two assistant keepers who would be needed to help run the signal. The price tag for these improvements was $29,000—about six times the original cost of the lighthouse.

In the meantime, the method of running the nation's lighthouse system was about to undergo a radical change. In 1910 the Lighthouse Board was dissolved and the Bureau of Lighthouses created. In the name of efficiency, a single man, George Putnam, was placed in charge and the United States' system of navigational aids re-evaluated. In the coming years the number of lights and buoys continued to grow, and many existing ones were upgraded.

In 1912 the fourth-order lens was installed, and Commander W. A. Moffett, inspector for the lighthouse district encompassing California, continued to recommend that a better fog signal be built. Though three thousand miles away, the Panama Canal, which was nearing completion, fueled the belief that northern Monterey Bay might yet become a major seaport. The expected increase in maritime shipping also renewed hopes that a breakwater might be built at Lighthouse Point to create an improved harbor.

The sea had long been one of Santa Cruz's most important assets. Each summer tens of thousands of tourists flocked here to enjoy the broad sandy beaches and colorful seaside amusements. In the winter, however, much of the town went into hibernation, this despite boasting of a year-round mild climate. Area businessmen hoped that a great seaport here would bring prosperity throughout the year.

It is no coincidence that the same year the Panama Canal opened, 1914, the present Santa Cruz Municipal Wharf was completed—a locally financed effort in part to coax the federal government into financing a breakwater. Although the shipment of lime and lumber from Santa Cruz was sharply declining, it was hoped that the wharf would serve as a terminus for goods brought from elsewhere in the state by railroad. Today the wharf, widened and largely catering to tourists, stands as the only portion of the "great seaport" dream to get off the drawing board. For the most part, ships continued to bypass Santa Cruz, and the city soon found it more profitable to rent dock space around the wharf to fishermen. Plans for a powerful fog signal at Lighthouse Point were likewise dropped.

The Santa Cruz lighthouse's newly-installed fourth-order Fresnel lens produced a unique flash sequence that assured mariners this was Santa Cruz and no place else. Each flash lasted 3½ seconds and was followed by an eclipse of 1½ seconds. Since the oil lamp had to burn continuously, a most ingenious device was used to make it appear to flash—a device a clock-maker would have been particularly proud of. Inside the stationary lens a pair of vertically-oriented opaque screens slowly revolved, alternately exposing and blocking out the light. The apparatus was powered by gravity. A 130-pound weight was attached to a half-inch clock cord wrapped around a six-inch drum. One winding set the screens revolving for six hours as the weight gradually descended through a drop tube below the lantern.

When Laura Hecox retired as keeper in 1916 the oil lamp

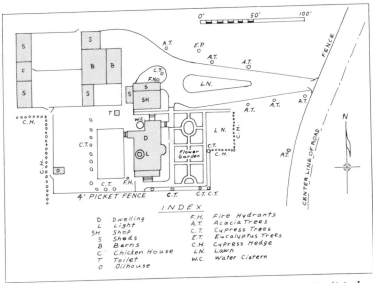

Part of map prepared by Keeper Arthur Anderson in 1921. (Modified from tracing in National Archives)

she had lovingly cared for through the many years was soon to follow. Miss Hecox knew the change was coming and, disliking change, was glad to have no part in it. During the 1916-17 fiscal year the Santa Cruz lighthouse, being small and in a town served by electric power, became one of the first in California to utilize an electric incandescent lamp. The new keeper, Arthur Anderson, eyed the 500-watt bulb with some suspicion at first, keeping one of the gasoline auxiliary lamps handy for emergencies. For a while the clock mechanism continued to be utilized, but eventually the electric light was simply turned on and off automatically to make the flashes.

Arthur C. Anderson, third and the last "real" keeper at the lighthouse, was a quiet, modest man, slim of build, and very proud of the rich heritage of the Lighthouse Service. Anderson was born in New York in 1873. After working for the War Department, he joined the Lighthouse Service in 1904 as a draftsman. He then moved to San Francisco and became chief draftsman there in 1907. Later he became a lighthouse inspector, his duty being to visit, often by small boat, the various lighthouses and make sure they were being properly maintained. Of course he had to know the workings of lighthouses inside and out. He was the ideal person for the job, being both a good observer and meticulous about details. However, he still found himself confined to his San Francisco office much of the time, inundated by paper work. Poor health forced him to look for a slower-paced job away from an office. When Laura Hecox resigned, the forty-four-year-old inspector accepted the keeper's job at Santa Cruz.

The Anderson era witnessed a number of improvements to the Santa Cruz light station. Additional buildings were erected for farm animals; trees and a flower garden were planted; and additions were built onto the lighthouse to provide quarters for a laborer to help with maintenance. In about 1931 workmen replaced the old lantern with a new one, slightly different in shape. In 1925 the government agreed to sell to the city for fifty dollars a twenty-foot-wide strip of land through the reservation for use a road. Conditions were that the city had to build within one year a concrete road at least five inches thick, install fences and gates as may be required by the government, and prohibit parking within the reservation. Prior to this, Cliff Drive was only a right-of-way through the reservation, negotiated in 1880.

"Nothing much ever happened around the lighthouse," said Anderson in a 1940 interview shortly before he retired. Nevertheless, there was occasional excitement at the point— sometimes tragedy. The keeper witnessed a number of drownings, some of them fishermen swept off the rocks by unusually large waves. The highest wind speed he ever saw was during the winter of 1937-38. "I figured the wind velocity on the point at seventy miles an hour." he recalled. "It took old cypress trees with a five-foot diameter and pulled them out of the ground as though they were tooth-picks."[26]

On July 1, 1939, another great administrative change (the third to play a role in the Santa Cruz lighthouse's history) swept through America's lighthouse system. Under one of President Roosevelt's reorganization plans, the Bureau of Lighthouses and its functions were transferred to and consolidated with the U.S. Coast Guard. The Coast Guard had been created in 1915 when the U.S. Life-Saving Service was combined with the Revenue-Cutter Service. The Lighthouse Service, which had survived as a separate entity of the federal government since George Washington's

Entrance to Santa Cruz lighthouse reservation, December, 1940. (Vester Dick Photography)

time, faded into the annals of history. In observance of the 150th anniversary of the Lighthouse Service, Congress proclaimed the week of August 7, 1939, "Lighthouse Week."

By this time there were about thirty thousand aids to navigation on the sea coasts, rivers, and lakes of the United States and its territories. This included fog signals, day marks, buoys, and over four hundred lighthouses. The Lighthouse Service had grown to an organization of 5,355 employees including 1,170 keepers and assistant keepers of lighthouses.

The demand for efficiency and economy which brought the administrative change was also to spell demise for many lighthouses over the coming years, one of the first of these being the one at Santa Cruz. Technology had reached the point where lighthouses, particularly small ones like the one at Santa Cruz, could be completely automated. This would save enormously on keepers' salaries and on building maintenance and supplies. The Coast Guard could afford to experiment with the Santa Cruz light since the shipping of goods to and from Santa Cruz by boat had ceased in the late 1930s. The light was now primarily only of use to local fishermen.

In February of 1941 the Coast Guard finished building a wooden framework tower about two hundred feet seaward of the old lighthouse. Atop the twenty-six-foot tower was placed a small lens-lantern controlled by an automatic timer. Compared to the 25,000 candlepower light that had radiated from the lighthouse, the lens-lantern yielded only 11,000 candlepower—further indication of Santa Cruz's decline as a seaport.

The Coast Guard had not yet divulged its plan for the lighthouse, but the implication was clear: just as the automatic light needed no keeper, with a new tower to support the light, the Coast Guard needed no lighthouse. Leaving the building vacant so near a populated area would only invite

Aerial view showing lighthouse, tower built to replace it, and old route of West Cliff Drive seaward of the tower, circa 1941.

Leonard Webb of the U.S. Coast Guard views a distant ship from the lighthouse gallery, December, 1940. (Vester Dick Photography)

squatters and vandalism. Several times life-saving equipment had been stolen from the point, once leaving Keeper Anderson helpless in preventing a drowning.

However, as fate would have it, the little white lighthouse, partly concealed by the sprawling branches of overgrown cypresses, had not quite outlived its usefulness. With the onset of World War II, plans to demolish the lighthouse were postponed. Instead, it became the home of Mr. and Mrs. N. E. Dowell and their daughter Lila. Mr. Dowell, who worked for the Coast Counties Gas and Electric Company, spent the remainder of his time maintaining the lighthouse and grounds. The reservation was frequently off limits to the public during the war years. Fox holes, connected by a maze of trenches, were dug into the point. From these, portable machine guns were aimed toward the Pacific. From the empty lighthouse lantern, men with binoculars kept careful watch over the bay and ocean, scanning the watery horizon for signs of enemy submarines or a surprise attack.

Anyone want to buy a lighthouse? That was the question posed by the Coast Guard in March of 1948. With the automatic light well established and the war over, the government called for bids for the purchase and removal of the lighthouse and other buildings. The deadline for the bidders was 2:00 P.M., April 14. When the letters were opened at the Coast Guard headquarters in San Francisco, the highest bidder turned out to be a Santa Cruz carpenter, Austin W. Furlow.

On May 20, 1948, Furlow and his son, Kenneth, began razing the house and surrounding buildings. The sturdy structure did not give in easily to the flailing hammers and crow bars. Heavy three-by-fours supported the walls, while three-by-ten inch timbers supported the first floor. Each day a small crowd of curious spectators gathered to watch the flurry of activity. Some came out of curiosity, others to buy wood or bricks. One couple came to purchase a single brick—as a memento they said. The eagle-topped flagpole went to a neighbor who erected it in his yard. By August the landmark was gone and the ground leveled. The following spring, green grass carpeted the site, at last erasing every trace of the buildings. Only the cypress trees, somewhat reduced in their ranks, guard the site today, the largest ones dating back to the Hecox era.

The Santa Cruz light was one of the first on the West Coast to be placed under automatic control. The final West Coast lighthouse to be automated, at Point Bonita on the north side of the Golden Gate, saw its last regular keeper in 1981. Fortunately, the lighthouses were often spared. Some have become museums, youth hostels, commercial buildings, or have been preserved by the National Park Service as at Point Bonita and Point Reyes. Others, however, have been sadly neglected and are in need of restoration.

Santa Cruz's unattended light was not without its problems. Vandals tampered with the beacon several times in later years, once doing several hundred dollars worth of damage. This forced the Coast Guard in 1965 to replace the attractive white picket fence surrounding the tower with a seven-foot-high cyclone fence topped by barbed wire.

Local fishermen complained that the light was too weak. They argued in a petition sent to the Coast Guard in December of 1959 that the light could hardly be distinguished from the headlamps of automobiles moving in the background along West Cliff Drive. In 1962 the Coast Guard replaced the 300-millimeter lens-lantern with a rotating aero-beacon of 80,000 candlepower.

In early 1941 this small lens-lantern on a wooden tower replaced the light in the lighthouse. (U.S. Coast Guard)

A New House for the Light

In the 1960s most people in Santa Cruz gave little thought to the fact that the place lacked a lighthouse—most except for Chuck and Esther Abbott. Mr. and Mrs. Abbott, who were professional photographers, moved to Santa Cruz in 1963. They had photographed many of America's lighthouses and, soon after arriving in Santa Cruz, set out to capture the Santa Cruz beacon. To their dismay, what they found resembled an oil derrick more than a lighthouse.

In December of 1965 the Abbotts announced that they wished to donate a lighthouse to the people of Santa Cruz, certainly one of the most unusual gifts in the town's annals. It was to be erected in memory of their eighteen-year-old son, Mark, who had drowned in February of that year while body surfing at Soquel Point, three miles east of Lighthouse Point. Money for the project would come from their late son's life insurance policy.

At first Mr. and Mrs. Abbott investigated the feasibility of reconstructing Santa Cruz's original lighthouse, but soon realized that the cost of building an entire dwelling would be prohibitive. Instead, a local firm, Ifland Engineering, was hired to design a small, brick building in keeping with some of the town's early-day houses. The result was unique and quite different architecturally from other West Coast lighthouses.

The Santa Cruz City Council responded enthusiastically to Mr. and Mrs. Abbott's proposal. Still, there were many details to be worked out with both the city and the U.S. Coast Guard. The Coast Guard approved the architect's

Mark Abbott Memorial lighthouse under construction, May 5, 1967. (Vester Dick Photography)

drawings in October of 1966. The location chosen was about thirty feet seaward of the framework tower then supporting the light. This, however, posed a problem. In its latter stages of construction, the new lighthouse would partially obstruct the light on the tower. This would not only pose some threat to boats leaving and entering Monterey Bay but would also be illegal under federal law. On the other hand, the Coast Guard could not move its light into the new lighthouse as agreed until construction was almost done. The problem was finally resolved by deciding to build the lighthouse more to the west and by the Coast Guard boosting the height of the framework tower until it was time to move the revolving light into its new home.

On a cold, rainy January 20, 1967, the Abbotts and city officials broke the ground for the new lighthouse. Construction began in March, and by the end of May the light sat on its new perch. Finishing touches were added during the summer in time for dedication in November. The Coast

Guard would continue to maintain the light, checking it periodically. The city accepted the responsibility of keeping up the building, which would also serve as a small nautical museum.

The seaward portion of the old lighthouse reservation (4.65 acres) had been deemed surplus by the federal government and was purchased by the city of Santa Cruz in 1960 for use as a public park. The government sold the land for $2,500, this being half the estimated fair market value at that time. However, a plot twenty feet square was retained for the tower. Interestingly, the government still owns the tiny plot, a precautionary measure should something ever go wrong with the privately-financed venture.

In the 1950s the landward part of the reservation (4.43 acres) belonged to the U.S. Army Reserve. The city acquired this property, also, in 1960 through a trade for land elsewhere. Later that year the city made an agreement with a developer from Santa Clara, Peter Pasetta, for him to build a hotel or apartment complex on the site. This was the first of several unsuccessful proposals to develop part of the old lighthouse reservation and the surrounding acreage which was once the Phelan estate. During the next two decades bitter controversy swept the surrounding community over whether or not a hotel and convention center should be built there. In 1980, under public pressure, the State of California purchased the land for a park. The state paid $5.7 million for a total of 28.2 acres, or roughly $200,000 per acre. Mr. and Mrs. Rountree, were they alive today, would undoubtedly be shocked. They had eagerly accepted $200 per acre from the government in 1868, then considered a respectable offer. Indeed the land has proven to be more valuable than the gold they were paid.

The Mark Abbott lighthouse, now surrounded by thirty-six acres of park land, is the youngest lighthouse in the

United States. It is also one of the very few built with private funds. Ironically, in this way it shares a link with the nation's oldest lighthouse, located at Sandy Hook, New Jersey. Erected in 1764, it was likewise privately financed. Perhaps the only other lighthouse built with private funds since the United States government went into the lighthouse keeping business in 1789 is the William Livingstone Memorial lighthouse on Belle Isle, Detroit.

The Abbott lighthouse, though the juvenile of America's lighthouse system, has still other links to the past. In an effort

In late May, 1967, the Coast Guard's light was moved to the new lighthouse. (Vester Dick Photography)

to give it some historical flavor, many materials from yester-
year were utilized in its construction, including some sixteen
thousand used bricks. Its wrought iron fence dates back to
California's gold rush era. Through the cooperation of the
U.S. Coast Guard, an octagonal lantern room was secured
which resembles that of the original Santa Cruz lighthouse.
This lantern was salvaged from the Oakland Harbor lighthouse which was built in 1903 and discontinued as a navigational aid in 1966. The rest of that lighthouse was later bought
and moved to 1951 Embarcadero Street in Oakland and
converted into a restaurant.[27]

Lighthouse Point's past has been shaped by trends visible
along much of the Monterey Bay coastline, the most important of these being transportation changes and increased
recreational use of the shoreline and bay. Where steamers
used to round the point, their holds filled with redwood
lumber or barrels of lime, surfers clad in wetsuits ride the
endless stream of breakers. Where horse-drawn buggies used
to bounce along a meandering cliff-side right-of-way, skaters,
bicyclists, and cars roll across asphalt and concrete. On the
nearby wharf, where railroad cars once transferred cargo to
steamers and where dozens of fishermen once docked, res-
taurants and gift shops now flourish. Cargo boats gave way
to fishing boats, which are giving way to pleasure boats. In
this trend lies the backbone of Santa Cruz's lighthouse
history.

In 1981 the name Lighthouse Field State Beach was adopted
for the new park. Later that year and in early 1982 public
meetings were held to decide what to do with it. In general
the consensus was to leave the park largely undeveloped,
adding only modest landscaping, wildlife observation areas,
picnic tables, and jogging trails. Today the light at the point
is not only a link in America's chain of lighthouses, but also a
link in a chain of California parks.

On November 22, 1967, local dignitaries gathered to congratulate
Mr. and Mrs. Chuck Abbott (foreground) at an informal lighthouse dedication ceremony. (Vester Dick Photography)

Notes

1. Herbert E. Bolton, *Spanish Exploration in the Southwest 1542-1706* (New York: Charles Scribner's Sons, 1916), p. 91.

2. U.S., Coast Survey, *Report of the Superintendent of the Coast Survey, showing the Progress of the Survey during the year 1852,* p. 105.

3. U.S., Congress, Senate, *Congressional Globe,* 32nd Cong., 1st sess., 1852, new series 152: 2457.

4. U.S., Coast Survey, *Report of the Superintendent of the Coast Survey, showing the Progress of the Survey during the year 1854,* pp. 220-221.

5. Ibid., 1855, p. 416.

6. Ibid., 1854, p. 221.

7. Ibid., p. 220.

8. Ibid.

9. Ralph C. Shanks, Jr. and Janetta Thompson Shanks, *Lighthouses and Lifeboats on the Redwood Coast,* p. 19.

10. "Important Land Decision," *Santa Cruz Sentinel,* 11 April 1868, p. 2.

11. "Abstract of Title to A. L. Rountree's lands at Santa Cruz, Cal.," Records of the U.S. Coast Guard, Record Group 26, Judicial and Fiscal Branch, National Archives, Washington, D.C.

12. "Light-House," *Santa Cruz Sentinel,* 26 June 1868, p. 2.

13. "Santa Cruz Lighthouse Interviewed," *Santa Cruz Sentinel,* 18 December 1869, p. 2.

14. "The New Light House," *Santa Cruz County Times,* 1 January 1870, p. 3.

15. Richard W. Updike, "Augustin Fresnel and His Lighthouse Lenses," *The Log of Mystic Seaport,* Spring 1980, p. 12.

16. Marie Valhasky [Catherine Brown], "The Story of Margaret M. Hecox," *Overland Monthly,* May 1892, p. 542.

17. Ibid.

18. Marie Valhasky [Catherine Brown], "The Story of Margaret M. Hecox II," *Overland Monthly,* July 1892, p. 100.

19. Ibid.

20. Arnold Burges Johnson, *The Modern Light-House Service* (Washington, D.C.: Government Printing Office, 1889), p. 106.

21. "Description of Light-House Tower, Buildings, and Premises at Santa Cruz Light-Station, Cal., June 30, 1907," Records of the U.S. Coast Guard, Record Group 26, Judicial and Fiscal Branch, National Archives, Washington, D.C.

22. "Santa Cruz Breakwater," *Santa Cruz Sentinel,* 26 March 1890, p. 2.

23. "The Lost Arch," *Santa Cruz Daily Surf,* 3 December 1888, p. 3.

24. J. Clifford Gallant, "Emily Fish, Keeper of Point Pinos Light-house," *Herald Weekend Magazine, Monterey Peninsula Herald,* 3 September 1978, pp. 4-8.

25. Johnson, *Light-House Service,* p. 56.

26. "Skip" Littlefield, "Santa Cruz Lighthouse, 72 Years Old, Becomes Relic Of S. C. History," *Santa Cruz Sentinel,* 1 January 1941, p. 8. December 1940 interview with Arthur Anderson.

27. Ralph C. Shanks, Jr. and Janetta Thompson Shanks, *Lighthouses of San Francisco Bay,* p. 109.

Sources

Fortunately for historians, lighthouses in this country have been in the care of the federal government since 1789. Thus, as one might expect, a huge volume of records have accumulated through these years. Among the published records that were most useful for this study were the annual reports of the U.S. Coast Survey, Lighthouse Board, and the Bureau of Lighthouses. Various years of the *Pacific Coast Pilot* were very helpful for their descriptions of the coastline and its lighthouses, particularly the monumental 1889 edition written by George Davidson. Old *Light Lists* provided an excellent year by year account of changes at the Santa Cruz light station. The *Congressional Globe* and the U.S. *Statutes at Large* were consulted for descriptions of congressional appropriations. Arnold Johnson's *The Modern Lighthouse Service* (Government Printing Office, 1889) gives an informative account of the nation's Lighthouse Establishment at that time and its history. George Weiss presents an equally valuable and detailed summary in his *The Lighthouse Service: Its History, Activities and Organization,* 1926 (reprinted by AMS Press, 1974).

The primary source of older, unpublished government documents on central California lighthouses is Record Group 26 in the National Archives at Washington, D.C., and San Bruno, California. Especially helpful for the Santa Cruz lighthouse were the descriptive pamphlets dated 1907 and 1917; clipping file; index to correspondence received by the Lighthouse Board; deed and abstract of title to the lighthouse site; register of keepers; and maps dated 1868 (two), 1879 (annotated in 1896), 1880, and 1921.

The United States Coast Guard, Twelfth District, Aids to Navigation Branch in San Francisco maintains excellent records of a more recent nature as well as a photographic file.

Among the newspapers gleaned for obituaries and coverage of noteworthy events were the *Santa Cruz Sentinel, Santa Cruz Surf, Santa Cruz Evening News, Santa Cruz County Times, Watsonville Pajaronian,* and *Monterey Peninsula Herald.* Relevant articles were found by scanning issues around likely dates and by searching the clipping files of institutions and individuals.

Many city and county records of Santa Cruz were searched including deeds, death certificates, minutes of city council meetings, correspondence files, and public works records.

For this study of Santa Cruz's lighthouses, every effort was made to use primary sources. Secondary accounts in books, magazines, and newspapers usually proved to be inaccurate. Unfortunately, the log books and guest register kept at the first lighthouse could not be located. Anyone knowing their whereabouts is urged to contact the Santa Cruz City Museum or the Santa Cruz County Historical Museum.

Further Reading

LIGHTHOUSES

Ehlers, Chad, and Gibbs, James A. *Sentinels of Solitude.* Portland, Oregon: Graphic Arts Center Publishing Co., 1981. Color photos with a short text.

Gibbs, James A. *Sentinels of the North Pacific.* Portland, Oregon: Binfords & Mort, 1955.

Gibbs, James A. *West Coast Lighthouses.* Seattle: Superior Publishing Co., 1974.

Holland, Francis Ross, Jr. *America's Lighthouses: Their Illustrated History Since 1716.* Brattleboro, Vermont: The Stephen Greene Press, 1972. *Must* reading for lighthouse enthusiasts.

Putnam, George R. "Beacons of the Sea," *National Geographic Magazine,* January 1913, pp. 1-53. Putnam headed the Bureau of Lighthouses for 25 years.

Putnam, George R. *Lighthouses and Lightships of the United States.* Boston: Houghton Mifflin Co., 1917.

Putnam, George R. "New Safeguards for Ships in Fog and Storm," *National Geographic Magazine,* August 1936, pp. 169-200.

Shanks, Ralph C., Jr., and Shanks, Janetta Thompson. *Lighthouses and Lifeboats on the Redwood Coast.* San Anselmo, California: Costaño Books, 1978. Both books by Ralph and Janetta Shanks are well-researched, well-illustrated, and well worth reading.

Shanks, Ralph C., Jr. and Shanks, Janetta Thompson. *Lighthouses of San Francisco Bay*. San Anselmo, California: Costaño Books, 1976.

Stick, David. *North Carolina Lighthouses*. Raleigh: North Carolina Department of Cultural Resources, Division of Archives and History, 1980.

Strobridge, Truman R. *Chronology of Aids to Navigation and the Old Lighthouse Service 1716-1939*. Washington, D. C.: Public Affairs Division, United States Coast Guard, 1974. A handy well-documented reference.

United States Coast Guard. *Historically Famous Lighthouses*. Washington, D. C.: U.S. Government Printing Office, 1972.

BIOGRAPHY AND REGIONAL HISTORY

Hecox, Margaret M. *California Caravan*. Edited and with introduction by Richard Dillon. San Jose, California: Harlan-Young Press, 1966. Similar to her account in the 1892 *Overland Monthly* article.

Perry, Frank. "California's Lighthousekeeper Naturalist," *Pacific Discovery*, September-October 1980, pp. 26-31. Biography of Laura Hecox.

Reinstedt, Randall A. *Shipwrecks and Sea Monsters of California's Central Coast*. Carmel, California: Ghost Town Publications, 1975.

Rowland, Leon. *Santa Cruz: The Early Years*. Santa Cruz: Paper Vision Press, 1980.

Santa Cruz County, California. Illustrations Descriptive of its Scenery, ... *With Historical Sketch of the County*. San Francisco: Wallace W. Elliott & Co., 1879. Includes biography of Adna A. Hecox.

Updike, Richard W. "Augustin Fresnel and His Lighthouse Lenses," *The Log of Mystic Seaport*, Spring 1980, pp. 10-14.

Mark Abbott Memorial lighthouse.